REALLY Stinky farts

U. STINKER

summersdale

Summersdale Publishers Ltd
46 West Street
Chichester
West Sussex
PO19 1RP
UK

www.summersdale.com

Printed and bound in Great Britain

ISBN: 1-84024-475-5
ISBN 13: 978-1-84024-475-5

REALLY

Stinky

fart

JOKES

He is so dumb he can't
fart and chew gum
at the same time.

Lyndon Baines Johnson
(about Gerald Ford)

Why couldn't the skeleton fart?

Because it didn't have the guts.

While waiting at the doctor's surgery, a man accidentally lets rip a really loud fart. He tries to look nonchalant and turns to the woman next to him as if nothing has happened. 'Do you have a copy of today's paper I could borrow?' he asks. 'No,' she replies, 'but if you put your hand out of the window you can rip some leaves off that bush.'

What smells and glows in the dark?

A Klingon fart.

REALLY
Stinky
fart
JOKES

FACT

Farts are gases escaping the body. You swallow gases in the air around you every time you drink or eat, especially if you wolf your meal down at breakneck speed. Your body also makes gas, and the best foods to eat for the ultimate stinker are onions, turkey, cabbage and Brussels sprouts.

In a certain Native American tribe, those who did the biggest farts were the most respected men in the village. One day, the chief finds that he can't break wind so he sends his messenger to the witch doctor for a remedy. 'Big chief no fart,' explains the messenger. He is given a bunch of herbs to add to the chief's meals to help but when this doesn't work, he is sent back again. 'Big chief no fart,' he says. This time he is given ten bunches of herbs, but the next day he returns with the same news, 'Big chief no fart.' At the end of his tether, the witch doctor sends him back to the chief with a sack full of herbs. The next day the messenger returns, 'Well?' demands the witch doctor, 'What happened?' The messenger looks at him and says solemnly 'Big fart, no chief.'

Laugh and the
world laughs
with you.

Fart and it will stop.

SONG

A fart is a musical instrument,

It comes from the island of bum,

It travels the valley of trouser-leg,

Whilst making a musical hum.

A man knocks on the door of his new girlfriend's house, nervously clutching a bunch of flowers. As soon as she opens the door, he realises that he really has to fart. Fortunately, she invites him to wait in the living room while she finishes getting ready. Feeling the need to let out a very big fart, he opens the living room door and lets off a huge stinker into the room. 'Phew, that was close,' he comments to himself before quickly shutting the door to contain the smell and waiting in the hallway for his girlfriend. She skips down the stairs just at the moment the living room door opens and two very uncomfortable-looking people walk out, with their hands over their noses. 'These are my parents,' says the girl brightly. 'I expect you met while I was getting ready?'

What's your farting style?

Simply find the day that you were born and discover what kind of a farter you are.

Monday – ENTHUSIASTIC

Will discuss his farts willingly and always looking to improve his performance.

Tuesday – ACCIDENT PRONE

Often ends up
following through.

Wednesday – NERVOUS

His louder farts
make him jump.

Thursday – MODEST

Always blames the dog.

Friday – ARROGANT

Always thinks that his farts are superior in noise and smell.

Saturday – CONNOISSEUR

Can detect what farters around him have eaten.

Sunday – NASTY

Eats beans and other fart-inducing foods on purpose before meetings and trips on public transport. And never opens the window.

As she is hoovering the boss's office, the cleaner does a fart that is so stinky that it makes her feel ill. Fortunately she has some floral scented polish amongst her cleaning products, so sprays it around the room to try and disguise the smell. Just then the boss walks in, having forgotten something. He sniffs the air in disgust. 'What is that?' he exclaims. 'It smells like someone had a dump in a flower bed!'

FACT

The average person
farts 14 times a day.

After dinner a man says to his wife, 'Why don't we try changing positions tonight?' 'OK,' she replies. His eyes light up. 'You go to the kitchen and clean up and I'll go and sit in the armchair, watch the football and fart.'

FACT

Whilst swearing loyalty to Queen Elizabeth I, the Earl of Oxford did a huge fart. He was so embarrassed that he left the country for seven years. When he returned, the Queen attempted to allay his self-consciousness. 'Oh, but I had quite forgotten the fart,' she said.

Promising her mum that she will be back by twelve, a girl goes down to the pub to meet her friends. After a few vodkas, she is persuaded to go clubbing so doesn't get home until four in the morning. As she is about to climb the stairs, the grandfather clock starts to chime. She knows that her mum would have heard the front door and would be awake so she decides to add on a few chimes of her own to make it seem as though it is midnight. In the morning, her mum remarks, 'I think we need to get someone to look at that clock. Last night it chimed four times, then there was a pause, a few strange grunting noises, and then a loud bang followed by a fart.'

In some social circles the matter of farting should be brought up with the utmost delicacy and discretion. Here are a few more descriptive terms to describe that most natural of habits:

Cutting the cheese

Unleashing a weapon of mass destruction

Playing the poo tuba

Committing an arse attack

Launching a pocket rocket

Choking a donkey

Stepping on a duck

Exploding a bomb between the cheeks

Blowing your own trumpet

Talking in Russian

Sneezing in your trousers

Killing the canary

What is a fart?

A royal salute,
heralding
the arrival of
Captain Turd.

There are three ladies in a waiting room. The first lady complements the second on her perfume and asks her what it is. 'A special blend, only available in France,' she replies haughtily. The first lady then announces that her perfume is unique, created just for her in a perfumery in Egypt. They look expectantly at the third, waiting for her contribution. She stands up and lets out a very stinky fart. 'Cauliflower curry,' she says proudly, 'from the Indian down the road.'

Confucius say: Man who fart
in church sit in own pew.

SONG

Beans, beans, good for your heart

The more you eat the more you fart

The more you fart the more you eat

The more you sit on the toilet seat!

Here are some alternative words for the product itself:

After dinner mint

Backdoor trumpet

Colon cologne

Curry cocktail

Nether belch

Poofume

Rectal turbulence

Talking trouser

Rumble of thunder

Rear end rumble

Thunder dumpling

Thunder and lightning
(when you follow through)

Did you hear about
the blind skunk?

He's dating a fart.

A teacher is taking her class on a school trip to the local museum. As they are waiting at the zebra crossing, she does a big loud fart. The children start to snigger so she turns to the boy next to her and says sharply, 'Stop that!'

'OK, Miss,' he replies, 'tell me which way it went and I will!'

REALLY Stinky
fart
JOKES

FACT

Farts can hit speeds of up to ten feet per second.

Passing a room in the maternity ward, a nurse overhears two relatives of an African patient having a debate. 'It's W-U-M-B-A' said the first. 'Wumba!' 'No, you are wrong,' said the second, 'it's moomba, spelt M-O-O-M-B-A. 'Don't you mean womb?' asks the nurse. 'Spelt W-O-M-B?' The two relatives look confused. 'Have you ever seen a hippo?' asks one of them. 'No,' replies the nurse.

'Well then,' he says, 'how on earth do you know what noise they make when they fart in the river?'

SONG

When you are sad, not everyone will see your tears...

When you are happy, not everyone will see your smile...

When you are angry, not everyone will see your frown...

When you lose your footing, not everyone will see you stumble...

But when you fart...

Ten Best Places to Fart

1. In a jacuzzi.

2. As you get off a really crowded train.

3. When there's a dog or a baby around to blame.

REALLY Stinky fart JOKES

4. On a roller coaster.

5. In a perfume shop.

6. In a theatre during the applause.

7. In a field full of cows.

8. Outside the Indian takeaway on a Friday night.

(Everyone else is at it too.)

9. In Tokyo.

(They wear masks there anyway
because of the pollution.)

10. Halfway through
a parachute jump.

Farts are a waste; with burps you can taste.

After spending over an hour preparing his dinner, a woman sits down at the table with her husband and starts to eat. 'You know I don't like lamb,' complains the husband, 'and these carrots aren't cooked enough.' She ignores him and carries on eating. After a few minutes he demands, 'Are you listening to me?' She looks up. 'No,' she replies, 'if I wanted to listen to an arsehole I would fart.'

FACT

The biggest farters in the world are termites.

Two flies were sitting on a dog turd. One farted and the other one turned to him and snapped, 'Do you mind? Can't you see I'm eating?'

A man is sitting in an American diner when the waitress comes over to take his order. 'I'll have some headlights please, two hubcaps and a pot of grease.' The waitress doesn't have a clue what he has just ordered so goes to ask the cook, who explains that he has used slang terms, and what he wants is two fried eggs on toast and a cup of coffee. The waitress goes back to the customer and serves him a plate of baked beans. 'I didn't order this!' he says. 'Well,' replies the waitress, 'I thought while you were waiting for your spare parts you could stock up on gas too.'

Ten Worst Places to Fart

1. Near an open flame.

2. In the cinema during a death scene.

3. As you are trying to pass the snacks trolley in an aeroplane aisle.

4. Whilst making confession.

5. At the dentist.
(He is supposed to be providing the gas, not you.)

6. In a submarine.
(Farting in small, airtight spaces will never make you popular.)

7. While closely following your abseil partner.

8. After saying 'I've had a lovely evening' on a first date.

9. During a full body search at customs.

10. Whilst having a bikini wax.

FACT

Chewing gum, not getting enough exercise, eating too quickly, drinking fizzy beverages and drinking through a straw can all contribute to excessive flatulence.

He who smelt it,

dealt it.

He who denied it,

supplied it.

He who detected it,

ejected it.

You said the rhyme,

you did the crime.

After suffering from flatulence all day, a woman called her husband to say she was leaving work. He asked her to wait a bit longer as he was cooking a special dinner and needed more time. A few hours later she went home, feeling very ill from all of the smelly farts that she was producing. When she got home he led her, blindfolded, into the dining room. Saying he was just going to serve up, he left her in the room. The poor woman couldn't contain the gas, and she farted three times in a row, each one smellier than the last. Fortunately the smell disappeared by the time her husband came back. He took off her blindfold… to reveal ten of her friends sitting in silence around the table.

King Louis XIV of France believed that it was a compliment to his visitors if he farted whilst talking to them.

REALLY Stinky **fart** JOKES

SONG

There once was a man from Shanghai

Whose farts could be heard in Dubai

When he felt one fermenting

There was no use lamenting

As he stuck out his bum and let fly

A boy is perching uncomfortably on the chair and when his mum asks him what the matter is, he replies, 'I have two problems. Firstly, my farts are sounding very strange, and I have a huge abscess on my bum. Do you think the two could be connected?' 'What kind of noises are your farts making?' asks his mum. 'Well, they kind of sound like HONDAA,' explains the boy. 'Ah yes,' says his mum nodding her head, 'if you make an appointment at the doctor to get the abscess cured it should solve that.' 'Why?' asks the boy. 'Because abscess makes the fart go hondaa!' she replies.

Farting in Other Languages

French: un pet

German: der Pups

Dutch: een wind laten

Hungarian: fing

Punjabi: pudd

Japanese: onara

How do you
make tear gas?

By eating baked
beans and onions.

One day a woman decided to trick her husband, who did a huge fart every single morning before getting up and leaving her in bed, choking on the smell. She had always warned him that he could fart his guts out like that but he paid her no attention. So one morning, as he rolled over after letting off a real stinker, she placed some uncooked tripe on the bed. She quickly went into the bathroom and a few minutes later heard a horrified yell. She returned and asked what the matter was. 'You were right!' he cried. 'I did fart my guts out! But don't worry,' he shifted uncomfortably and pulled his hand out from under the duvet, 'they're back in now!'

Top Five Alternative Book Titles

James and the Giant Fart

Animal Fart

Pride and Flatulence

The Complete Farts of Shakespeare

The Curious Incident of the Fart in the Night time

REALLY Stinky
fart JOKES

FACT

About eight per cent
of New Zealand's
greenhouse gas
emissions are caused
by animal farts.

SONG

Farting can be fun
Be it silent or loud
You can do it on the run
You can do it in a crowd.
Some are very dry
And some are very wet
Some can make you cry
And some will make you sweat.
So eat some spicy food
And try to let one through
Yes, farting's very rude
But it's awfully funny too!

Two sisters go to visit their elderly mother in a private hospital. They have paid a lot of money and they are hoping that she is receiving good care. They find that the nurses are very friendly and attentive and there is always someone around to help. For instance, as the women sit chatting with their mother they notice that every time she shifts in her chair, a nurse rushes over to gently straighten her up. Both daughters are happy that they made the right choice of hospital and later ask their mother what she thinks of the place. She replies, 'Oh, it's very nice. They are friendly and do everything they can to help. There's only one complaint — I'm dying to do a fart, but every time I get ready to let one off they force me to suck it back up.'

Top Five Alternative Film Titles

Fartspotting

Raiders of the Lost Fart

Lethal Fart

Robin Hood Prince of Farts

*On Her Majesty's
Secret Fart*

What's faster
than the speed of
light and smells
of cheese?

Mighty Mouse farts.

Miss Brown is teaching her English class to incorporate new words into their sentences. She asks one little boy to give an example of a sentence using the word 'undoubtedly'.

'Should farts make your trousers wet and lumpy?' he asks.

'Of course not, now please just make a sentence,' answers Miss Brown.

'Well then,' replies the pupil, 'I have undoubtedly pooed my pants.'

Top Five Alternative Song Titles

'Brown-fart Girl'

'Dancing Fart'

'I've Had the Fart
of My Life'

'Oops I Farted Again'

'Born to Fart'

FACT

When people die, the mortician has to perform a special kind of massage on the corpse's body in order to release any gas that may be still in the gut. People can still fart for a short time after death and families and friends would not appreciate the lingering gases being released during the funeral.

Why did Hansel let off big smelly farts all the way back from the gingerbread house?

So his deaf and blind sister Gretel wouldn't lose her way.

REALLY Stinky fart JOKES

A shopkeeper greets a customer, who asks him where the toilet rolls are. 'Here you go,' says the shopkeeper. 'Did you want blue, peach, primrose yellow…?'

'White will do,' replies the man. 'I prefer to colour it myself.'

FACT

Most farts are done by
women. They fart three
times more during the
day than men do.

Alternative Names for Farters

Bugle bum

Fartmeister

Methane maker

Organ arse

Snorkeldorfer
(an underwater farter)

During a meeting between three international companies, the Chinese representative holds his hand up near his face and starts muttering.

'What are you doing?' asks the English representative curiously.

'I'm recording some notes. I have a microchip implanted in my hand,' replies the Japanese man.

Then the German representative takes out what looks like a credit card, and starts tapping on it with his fingers. 'Just telling my secretary to change my flight booking,' he explains. 'This is the latest in communications technology.'

Then the Englishman shifts in his seat and there is a fart-like noise. 'Excuse me,' he says cheerfully, 'just received an e-mail.'

FACT

During the reign of the Roman Emperor Claudius, a law was passed making it legal to fart at banquets. Although people thought it was more polite to try to hold their farts in, the popular medical opinion at the time was that this could be harmful, and therefore it was thought that the public should be encouraged to let the gas go.

REALLY
Stinky
fart
JOKES

How do you know
if a woman is
wearing tights?

When she farts you
can see bubbles
all down her leg.

A woman goes to see the doctor and explains that she can't stop farting. 'It's not a huge problem because they don't smell or make a noise, but I just want them to stop. I mean, since being in this office I have already farted a few times but you haven't noticed. Can you prescribe me something?'

The doctor takes out his notebook and writes something down.

'Great, are you writing me a prescription?' she asks.

'Yes, I'm prescribing some decongestants for your nose,' replies the doctor, 'and I'm also making a note to get you an appointment for a hearing test.'

REALLY Stinky
fart
JOKES

FACT

The Canelos tribe in Ecuador believe that every time someone farts, their soul escapes, and this can only be prevented by slapping the farter on the back. As punishment for farting, members of the tribe have to prepare a meal for everyone else.

A young woman is invited to her company's summer party, at the boss's house. She has only been working with the company for a month, so she is very nervous. After the meal, she lets off a big noisy fart, much to her embarrassment. But when the boss stands up and shouts at his dog, who is sitting by her feet, she thinks she has got away with it. When she farts a second time a few minutes later, she hopes that he will blame the dog again. Indeed he starts to shout at the dog, 'Go away Charlie! Away!' The dog doesn't move so she relaxes and when she feels another huge fart coming on, she is happy to let it out. 'Charlie,' shouts the boss, 'get away from her; she'll crap all over you next!'

REALLY Stinky fart JOKES

FACT

Every day you inhale
1 litre of other
people's fart gases.

Why did the
cantankerous old
man take toilet
paper to the
party with him?

Because he was
a party pooper.

A husband and wife are lying in bed when the man does a big noisy fart. 'One nil!' he exclaims gleefully. In response, the old lady rolls over and does a huge fart in his direction. 'One all!' she shouts. This carries on until the score is three all. It is the old man's turn but try as he might, he cannot fart. He tries so hard that he ends up following through in the bed. Before his wife notices he shouts, 'Half time! Switch sides!'

FACT

The longest recorded fart had a duration of 2 minutes and 42 seconds.

Farts are much like snowflakes: no two are ever the same. Most, however, will fall into one of the following categories, and anyone who's ever launched a pocket rocket will recognise their favourites in the following...

The Frightening Fart

Easily identified, this fart will start as an eerily high note before ending abruptly with a much lower sound. This finish is the reason for the frightening nature of this fart; it almost certainly indicates a situation that is a cause for concern. This type of fart can frighten not only the farter, but also those in close proximity.

The Increasing Fart

These farts start off normally but, depending on the surface on which the farter is sitting, their volume increases. Empty oil barrels can encourage the ultimate increasing fart, as metal is an effective amplifier.

The Bubbling Fart

This is one of the most self-indulgent type of fart, usually because it occurs in the bath where the farter is likely to be alone and can therefore enjoy it without the concern of any social implications. Farting in the bath will always produce bubbles and, if you are really lucky, you may be able to produce an Increasing Fart at the same time.

The Olympic Fart

As the name suggests, the performance of this fart is a very special event that doesn't happen very often, perhaps only once every four years. Best when in a silent yet crowded place, such as in church just before the sermon starts, this is a huge fart that will reach everybody's ears, and probably most people's noses. A fart on this scale will always result in everybody turning around to locate the perpetrator, and is guaranteed to impress the crowd.

The Hidden Fart

The aim of this fart is to camouflage the fart noise behind another sound, such as a cough, the scraping of a chair along the floor or the slamming shut of a heavy book. For this fart to work the timing has to be exact, but as this is rarely possible to achieve, the attempt to do so often leads to all sorts of embarrassment or amusement,

depending on whether you are
the farter or the onlooker.

The Firework Fart

A veritable concert of farting, this one is easily identified by the sheer number and variety of noises it creates. They will mostly consist of pops and bangs and just when you think the display has finished, a huge fart will explode that puts all the others in the shade. A very uncommon fart, but if in friendly company, this can easily earn the farter some applause.

The Unidentifiable Fart

This type of fart produces a stink but arrives without a peep. A professional will usually let rip with this one in substantial crowds of people, and therefore identifying the culprit can be difficult. Key signs to look out for are a red face, whistling and staring around the room in a shifty manner.

The British Fart

Its short and brisk notes distinguish this fart, and its entrance is never acknowledged. Anyone within earshot must maintain a stiff upper lip and carry on with what they are doing without raising an eyebrow.

The Questioning Fart

The tone of this fart takes an upward incline and as a result sounds uncertain of itself. Also known as 'the Australian Fart'.

The Punctuation Fart

This rare fart has to be extremely well timed but when done correctly, those in company are in for some real flatulence fun. A quick, loud fart at the end of a statement or command is an extremely effective way to make a point. For example, an enthusiastic 'Cheers' followed by an equally enthusiastic expulsion of gas will ensure that particular celebration will never be forgotten.

Did you know
diarrhoea is
hereditary?

Yes – it runs in
your jeans!

What do you call a man with diarrhoea who attempts a fart?

Brave.

FACT

When a fart is being created, it reaches a temperature of nearly 100 degrees Fahrenheit.

A girl goes to the doctor and says she has an embarrassing problem. 'I am a ballerina,' she explains, 'but every time I dance I can't stop farting. It is so embarrassing.' The doctor tells her to give him a demonstration so she dances for about five minutes, all the while letting out big, noisy and smelly farts. 'Can you help me?' she asks. 'I think so,' replies the doctor, bending over. When he stands

up she sees that he is holding
a long metal pole with a hook
on the end. 'What's that for?'
she cries, looking panicked.
'Opening the window,' he says,
'I can't breathe in here.'

SONG

Peaches, peaches, I smell peaches,

Yonder goes a boy with a
hole in his breeches

Three Eskimos are arguing over whose igloo is the coldest, so they decide to put each other's claims to the test. They go to the first Eskimo's igloo and he holds a cup of water above his head and pours the water out. When an ice block forms in mid air, the other two are impressed, but still insist that their igloos are colder. In the second, the Eskimo lights a cigarette and when he exhales, the smoke coming out of his nose freezes. The third Eskimo promises his friends something even more impressive. At his igloo, he goes straight to the bed, and from underneath the furs he pulls out a small cube of ice. He holds it between his fingers and puts a lighter underneath. Almost immediately a horrible smell fills the room, followed by a loud PHHRUUP!

REALLY Stinky **fart** JOKES

FACT

Eighty-one months of
constant farting by one
person will produce the
same amount of energy
as a nuclear bomb.

A woman walks into a very expensive shoe shop to admire the display. Leaning over to pick up a particularly beautiful pair of high-heeled shoes, she accidentally lets out a fart. Seeing no one around, she thinks she has got away with it. Just then a salesman walks up to her and asks if she would like any assistance. She asks about the price of the beautiful shoes. 'Well madam,' he replies, 'if just touching them makes you fart, you are going to poop your panties when you find out how much they cost.'

Every man likes the
smell of his own farts.

Icelandic proverb

Also Available

REALLY DAFT IDEAS

D. I. SASTER

£4.99

Paperback

Some ideas should never have made it further than the half-witted minds they originated from. *Really Daft Ideas* picks out the pottiest true stories to make you laugh and cringe.

From the soldier who tied a hammock between two wall lockers, only to be fatally crushed by them at bedtime, to the man who took aim at a spider crawling up his leg and shot himself instead, this book demonstrates why it's a good idea to think before you act.

REALLY

GROSS FACTS

EVERYTHING YOU DON'T NEED TO KNOW BUT CAN'T RESIST READING ABOUT

TED LEECH

REALLY GROSS FACTS

TED LEECH

£2.99

Paperback

What grosses you out? How about this:

- Attila the Hun died from drowning in his own nosebleed.
- The best recorded distance for projectile vomiting is 8 metres.
- One pound of peanut butter can contain up to 150 bug fragments and five rodent hairs.

This crusty, thoroughly distasteful and utterly compelling book of facts will disgust your friends and give hours of revolting, sickening pleasure.

BORED STUPID

A. FIDGET

£2.99

Paperback

Sand a mushroom... Ring McDonald's and complain about the food... Write a book about a previous life... Polish the ceiling... Plait your dog's hair... Wash a tree.

Bored to tears? On the bus, in a lecture, at home or at work, let's face it: life can be mind-numbingly boring sometimes.

Brighten up your drab and wholly pointless life with these brainless and completely daft things to do.

www.summersdale.com